HOUGHTON MIFFLIN

Reading

A Legacy of Literacy

American Stories

HOUGHTON MIFFLIN

BOSTON • MORRIS PLAINS, NJ

California • Colorado • Georgia • Illinois • New Jersey • Texas

Design, Art Management and Page Production: Kirchoff/Wohlberg, Inc.

ILLUSTRATION CREDITS
4-21 Bill Farnsworth. **22-27, 29-30, 33-39** Cedric Lucas. **40-57** Katie Keller. **58-75** Garin Baker.

Printed in U.S.A.

ISBN: 0-618-04399-3

6789-VH-05 04 03 02

American Stories

Contents

The Math Bee

by Delores Lowe Friedman
illustrated by Bill Farnsworth

Strategy Focus

When Portia competes in a school math bee, can you **predict** who will be her biggest supporters?

Saturdays were always busy at the Gordon house. Mom was up and out to work just as the sun began to fill the sky. When Dad woke Portia at nine, she pulled the covers over her head.

"Just let me sleep a little longer," she begged.

"Chores!" said Dad.

Portia did the dusting. Dad mopped the kitchen floor. Cleaning with Dad was fun because he always made up funny games to pass the time.

"Suppose you had four arms," he said, with a gleam in his eye.

"How many fingers would I have? Twenty," she said before Dad could continue.

"Good answer, but I was thinking you could dust two times faster, and you sure would be funny-looking," Dad said.

"Oh, Dad," Portia said with a sigh.

Just then the phone rang. Dad answered it.

When Dad hung up, he said, "Portia, I have to go to the airport. They're having some trouble landing the planes. Why don't you come with me?"

"Is it dangerous, Dad?" asked Portia. "Is a plane going to crash?"

"No, honey. I just have to look at some numbers and figure some things out," Dad answered.

At the airport they drove right to the control tower.

Inside were huge windows where the air traffic controllers could watch the planes they were guiding.

"Look over there," said Dad as he pointed out a window. "A plane will land on that runway in exactly three minutes."

Portia looked back out at the runway. Before she knew it, there was the plane!

Portia said, "Wow, how did you know?"

"I knew how high up the plane was, how fast it was going, and how long it usually takes for a plane to land," answered Dad. "Just a big math problem, really."

On Monday, Miss Frew told Portia's class, "Next month the school is having a math bee for the fourth-grade classes. It will be like a spelling bee, but with math problems."

I love math, Portia thought. I hope I can be in it.

"I think a team from our class can win," Miss Frew said. "If we do, we'll have a pizza party!"

"That sounds great, Miss Frew," said Portia. "I want to be on the team, but I don't think I know how to win."

"That's okay," said Miss Frew. "I'll be your coach. The math team can come to school early every morning, and we can study together."

When Portia got home, Mom was in the kitchen. "How are you, sweetie?" she said.

"I'm great," said Portia. "We're having a math bee in school. Miss Frew said she would help us study."

"Your father won the math medal in high school. You should ask him to help you study, too."

For the next several weeks, Portia got up early each morning. She hurried to school to work with three other students and Miss Frew.

Miss Frew taught them many math tricks and shortcuts. She taught them to do math problems in their heads and to work as fast as possible.

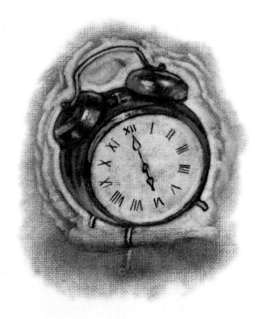

The night before the math bee, Dad helped Portia do the hardest problems she had ever done. When she solved the last one, she asked, "Did I get it right?"

"What do you think?" he asked.

"I'm pretty sure I did. The answer just makes sense."

Then Dad took out a ribbon with a medal on it. "I want you to have this," he said.

"But Dad, this is your medal, and we haven't won the math bee yet."

"I think you have earned it," Dad said, "for all the hard work you did this month. When you work hard and do your best, you're a winner."

The next day, just before the contest, Miss Frew told the team, "You are ready. You studied hard. Just do your best, and you'll be winners!"

Just what Dad said! thought Portia.

Portia stood close to her teammates on one side of the stage. The other fourth-grade team stood on the other side. The teams took turns solving problem after problem. Finally, the other team gave a wrong answer. If Portia and her teammates solved the problem correctly, they would win. The auditorium was very quiet.

Portia and her teammates worked out the problem. Portia called out the answer.

"That's right!" Mrs. Jackson shouted.

"Pizza party!" shouted Portia's class.

"Count me in!" said Portia.

Dr. Portia B. Gordon-Ketosugbo grew up in Queens, New York. She loved math as a little girl and enjoyed doing problems with her father, who was an award-winning aeronautical engineer. Her fourth-grade teacher encouraged math skills with contests and competitions. Portia decided to use her love of math in the field of chemistry. She is now the director of research for a major pharmaceutical company.

Responding

Think About the Selection

1. Where does Portia's father work?

2. What is the difference between a spelling bee and a math bee?

3. When does Dad give Portia his medal?

What Happens Next?

Copy the chart on a piece of paper. Write these events from the story in order on the chart:

Portia's team wins the math bee.

Portia and Dad go to the airport.

Portia gets chosen for the math bee.

Portia helps Dad with chores.

Story Events
1. Portia helps Dad with chores.
?
?
?

A Breath of Fresh Air

By Rhonda Rodriguez
illustrated by Cedric Lucas

Strategy Focus

As you read about Javi's first trip out of the city, stop once in a while to **evaluate** how well the author shows Javi adjusting to country life.

"July 7, 1959. Today I see the world," Javi Perez wrote in his diary.

Then Javi looked out the window of the train. It sped through the mountains, and all he could see were trees. He'd never been more than ten blocks away from his apartment before. But today he was traveling a hundred miles away from home to stay with a family he had never met. Javi was to be part of the Fresh Air program. It matched city kids with country families for two weeks during the summer.

Javi's mother thought he was too young to be part of the Fresh Air program. She didn't want him to go that far away. But Javi knew that age nine was old enough for an adventure. Just imagine, he thought. Two whole weeks of fun. He wouldn't have to help Mami do the laundry, babysit for his little sister, Rosa, or make sandwiches in Tía Lola's deli.

It was a long trip. Finally, the conductor called out "Northboro." Javi stepped onto the platform. The train pulled out of the station. No one was there to greet him. Have they forgotten about me? Javi wondered. Just then a station wagon turned into the parking lot. A woman leaned out the driver's window.

"You must be Javi," she said. "I'm Marge Harris. I'm so glad you're here! Your room's all ready, and dinner's waiting."

"My own room?" Javi asked in surprise. Then he remembered his manners and said, "It's great to meet you, Mrs. Harris. Thank you for inviting me to your home."

"You are entirely welcome, Javi," Mrs. Harris said. "Your room is in the attic, but it's all yours. Now let's get home before the food gets cold."

The Harrises' front yard was bigger than the yards of five houses in Brooklyn put together. What do they do with so much space? Javi wondered. Then Mrs. Harris opened the front door, and a giant dog knocked Javi flat on his back and started licking his face.

"Cypress, get off now! Be nice!" Mrs. Harris said. The dog backed away, but Javi was still nervous. The dogs he knew in Brooklyn were half the size of this one.

The house was quiet. "The boys are still at Little League, but they'll be home soon," Mrs. Harris said. "Dinner's still warm. Have as much as you want. Do you want to eat in here or in the TV room?"

Javi blinked, not sure what to say. At home, his family ate dinner together. Mami made rice and beans, sometimes with chicken. Sometimes Papi brought home extra cod cakes from his job at the fish market.

That night in his cozy attic room, Javi lay wide awake. At first he thought about the Harrises. They were so nice! He had met Joey, Ricky, and their father when they came home from Little League.

After a while, Javi tried to fall asleep. But it was too quiet. The only sound was crickets chirping. In Brooklyn, he could hear cars, radios, TVs, and conversations from the street. And Javi didn't know having a room of his own would be so lonely. Finally, he was so tired that he fell asleep.

The next morning he woke up with several itchy, red mosquito bites. He went down to the kitchen. Mrs. Harris was having breakfast. She said, "Oh, Javi, the mosquitoes had a feast last night! Some lotion will take the itch away."

Soon, Javi had circles of crusty pink lotion on his face. He tried not to scratch them. He looked funny. He wanted to go home.

That afternoon, Javi followed Joey and Ricky down the road to town. They walked by a farm, and Javi held his nose. "What's that awful smell?"

"Haven't you ever seen a cow before?" Joey said.

"I've seen them, but I haven't smelled them," Javi said.

"Do you know why the brown cows are brown?" Ricky asked.

"Chocolate milk?" Javi joked.

They all laughed. "You're all right, for a city kid," Joey said, clapping him on the shoulder.

Soon they were at a house with a yard even
bigger than the Harrises'. A whole bunch of kids
were there. An older boy named Stu was picking
teams to play baseball.

"Put Javi on my team, Stu," Joey said.

"Okay with me," Stu agreed. "But are you sure you want him? He doesn't even have a glove."

Javi scowled. He'd show Stu. "I don't need a glove!" he said. "I'll show you a REAL game we play back home in Brooklyn. It's called stickball. We don't need gloves or bats or anything."

The kids accepted Javi's dare. Before long, they had found a thick tree branch to hit with. They used their T-shirts as bases. Stu pitched the ball, and Javi slammed it out to left field, running the bases in record time.

"Hey, why didn't you tell us that you're the best stickball player in Brooklyn?" said Stu.

"Only the best on my block," said Javi, with a smile.

They played stickball all afternoon. The other kids asked him lots of questions.

"Is it true that you can see all the way to Europe from the top of the Empire State Building?"

"Do you go to *all* the Yankee games?"

"Are you scared to ride on the subway?"

Javi couldn't believe it. They knew as little about New York City as he knew about Northboro!

Javi was in such a good mood by the end of the day that he forgot how much he itched. He even let Cypress lick him hello when he, Joey, and Ricky got home. "How about hamburgers for dinner tonight?" Mrs. Harris asked.

"YES!" said all three boys.

Javi smiled. He was going to like Northboro just fine.

Responding

Think About the Selection

1 Where do the Harrises live?

2 Name two clues that tell you this story happens many years ago.

3 If Ricky visits Javi, what might Javi show him in New York City?

Making Inferences

Copy this character study on a piece of paper. Read what the author says about the character. Then use the clues to write what you can figure out about the character.

Character Study for Javi Perez	
What the author says:	**What you can figure out:**
Javi says "Thank you."	Javi is polite.
Javi can't sleep.	?
Javi makes a joke about cows.	?
Javi says he's the best stickball player on his block.	?

TWO COLD EARS

by Kitty Colton
illustrated by Katie Keller

Strategy Focus

As you read, **summarize** each part of the story. Tell about what happens in your own words.

This is the story of how two cold ears lead to one big idea.

The ears belong to Chester Greenwood. Chester lived in Farmington, Maine, more than a hundred years ago. Some things were a lot different in those days.

But other things were pretty much the same.
Take the weather. From early fall to late spring,
Farmington had only three kinds of weather:
cold, colder, and coldest.

Chester loved the cold weather because it meant snow to sled on and ice to skate on. But there were two things about winter Chester didn't like at all: his ears.

You see, Chester had problem ears. They
got so cold they ached. They turned colors,
too — from white to red to blueberry blue. Hats
didn't cover them. Wool mufflers made them itch.

44

Chester tried everything he could think of. But nothing worked. No matter what he tried, his ears were always cold, colder, coldest.

But cold ears couldn't hold Chester back. Nothing held Chester back.

That boy was always bursting with smart notions.

As a young sprout, he did odd jobs for the neighbors. He gave the money he earned to his ma and pa.

When he was twelve, Chester sold eggs from his family's farm. He used the money to buy candy. Now, most kids would eat that candy. Not Chester. (Well, maybe a piece or two.) He sold it and gave the money to his family.

In 1873, Chester turned fifteen. His ma and pa gave him new ice skates. He rushed through his chores, and then he raced to Abbot Pond.

It was one of the coldest days of the year. The weather was swell for skating but not for ears. Chester yanked his hat down as far as it would go. He stepped on the ice. Right off, his ears started throbbing like toothaches.

Chester clapped his hands to his ears. Then he fell — splat! — on the ice. That's when the big idea knocked itself into his head.

As fast as he could, Chester took off for home.

Chester found two pieces of wire. He bent them into circles. Then he found some scraps of fur and fabric. He asked his grandma to help him. She sewed beaver fur on the outside of each circle. On the inside, she sewed soft black velvet.

Then Chester hung the circles from his hat.

Chester put on the hat.
Ta-da!
His ears felt warm, warmer, warmest.
He raced out the door. He couldn't wait to try out his new invention.

Back at Abbot Pond, Chester's friends called to him. "Hey, Chester! What have you got on your ears?"

Chester yelled back, "My ear protectors!"

Everybody laughed and pointed. "Who'd
want to wear those silly things?" they shouted.

Well, as it turned out, lots of people wanted to wear Chester's ear protectors. Pretty soon, everybody in Farmington wanted a pair. Then people all over the world wanted them.

Chester built a factory to make his ear
protectors. And Chester being Chester, he kept
working to make them better.

He attached them to a bent strip of metal.
He made the name better too. He called them
"earmufflers."

Nowadays, Farmington is proud of its famous inventor. Every winter, folks gather to celebrate Chester Greenwood Day. There's an earmuff fashion show and a big parade. Of course, everybody wears earmuffs — even dogs, horses, and fire engines!

Responding

THINK ABOUT THE SELECTION

1 What did Chester call his invention at first?

2 How do you think Chester feels when he gets his new skates?

3 The author writes that nothing held Chester back. What does the author mean by "nothing"?

MAKING GENERALIZATIONS

Copy the chart on a piece of paper and answer the questions.

WHAT DOES THE AUTHOR MEAN BY "EVERYBODY" WHEN SHE WRITES	
Everybody in Farmington wanted a pair.	?
Everybody wears earmuffs, even dogs, horses, and fire engines!	?
Everybody laughed and pointed.	All of Chester's friends who were at the pond

Two-Star Day

by Veronica Freeman Ellis

illustrated by Garin Baker

Strategy Focus

It's a big day for Tonieh and his family. As you read, think of **questions** to ask Tonieh and his family about their day.

On Friday morning, Tonieh N'Da looked at the calendar on the kitchen wall. It was a two-star day.

First of all, it was Tonieh's birthday.
Second, it was the day his parents and sister
would become United States citizens.

Tonieh was already a citizen because he was born in the United States. His parents and sister were born in the Ivory Coast, in Africa.

People who become citizens must know United States history. So all winter long, Tonieh tested his family to get them ready for their citizenship ceremony.

"How many stars were on the first flag?" Tonieh asked.

"Thirteen for the thirteen colonies," his mother said.

"Who was the third president?" he asked.

"Thomas Jefferson," his father said.

"Who wrote 'The Star-Spangled Banner'?" Tonieh asked.

"Francis Scott Key," said his sister, Tanya.

Thomas Jefferson

Francis Scott Key

So now the day had arrived.

Tonieh waited with his family until they
were called into another room.

Tonieh spent the time watching people come
and go.

Sometimes a man or a woman was called.
Sometimes it was a whole family. They all came
back holding a piece of paper.

At last Tonieh's family came back with theirs.

Now it was time to take the oath of citizenship.
Tonieh stood with everyone as the judge entered.
His family and the others raised their right hands.
Now they were all citizens.

The judge spoke to the new citizens. She said that being a citizen of the United States is an honor. She told people over eighteen that they can vote. She said that citizens can serve on a jury and work for the government.

After the ceremony, the N'Da family went out for lunch. Everybody ordered their favorite dish. The best part was when the cake was served.

"Happy birthday to you!" said Tonieh's mother.

"Happy Citizen's Day to you!" said Tonieh.

"You were in that other room for a long time," said Tonieh.

"We took reading tests," said Tanya.

"We took writing tests, too," said Tonieh's mother. "Everyone who becomes a citizen takes those tests."

"Why?" asked Tonieh.

"To show we can read and write English," said his father.

"What did you read?" Tonieh asked.

"We read pages from a history book,"
said Tanya.

"What did you write?" asked Tonieh.

"I wrote about voting," said Tonieh's mother.
"I wrote about being on a jury," said his father.
"I wrote about people who become citizens,"
said Tanya.

That night, Tonieh felt lucky. Nine years ago, he was born a citizen of the United States. Next year, when he celebrated his tenth birthday, his family would celebrate their first year as citizens. It would be another two-star day!

Tonieh couldn't wait.

Think About the Selection

1 What country is Tonieh's family from?

2 How do you know Tonieh's family can now read and write English?

3 What happens because it is Tonieh's birthday? What happens because Tonieh's parents and sister are becoming citizens?

Categorize and Classify

Copy the chart on a piece of paper. Complete the chart by writing facts from the story for each category.

New Citizens Must:	New Citizens Over 18 May:
know history	vote
?	?
?	?